SHARKS

written by M Oakley
illustrated by S Boni *and* L R Galante

Ladybird

CONTENTS

Lateral line
A sensory line, that picks up vibrations from other fish.

Dorsal fin
The familiar triangular-shaped fin on a shark's back helps a shark to balance in water.

Pectoral fin
This fin, one either side of a shark's body, is used for steering and braking.

THREE THREATENING ONES

Several species of shark
have been known
to attack
people. As well
as great white
sharks, tiger sharks
and bull sharks are
considered a danger. Bull
sharks hunt in tropical seas
and have even been known to
swim up freshwater rivers and even
into lakes. However, there is still more
chance of being struck by lightning than being
attacked by these sharks.

Sometimes
sharks gather,
mysteriously, in
large packs. Some
of the biggest shark
gatherings occur off the
Central American coastline.

A SHARK'S BODY

Eye
Shark's eyes
have a special
reflective lens
to help them
see in the dark.

Muscle
Arranged in narrow
zigzag strips.

Snout

Nostril

Teeth
Fearsome rows of
teeth in the jaws.

Sensitive pores
These enable sharks to
detect weak electrical
impulses and help to
locate prey.

Gills
Oxygen from the water
passes into the shark's
bloodstream through
the gills.

WATER BABIES

When mating, a male shark grasps its partner with its teeth, sometimes causing cuts and gashes. These usually heal up very quickly. At birth, sharks are strong enough to look after themselves. Interestingly, sharks have three different methods of reproducing.

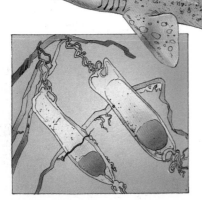

Egg layers
Many sharks, like the dogfish, hatch from eggs which are laid by the mother. The eggs are protected by a tough, leathery casing.

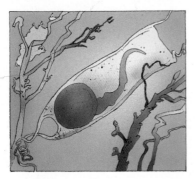

A shark develops inside each egg with its own food supply – the egg-sac. As the baby shark grows, the egg-sac shrinks. This takes about nine months.

Then, the baby shark searches for the weakest point in the egg case and forces its way out to freedom – a perfect miniature adult shark.

Caudal fin

Provides the power for swimming. Its distinctive shape is often used to identify kinds of shark.

Asymmetric tail

A shark swims by moving its tail from side-to-side. The upper lobe of a shark's tail is larger than the lower one. This helps the shark to move up and down as well as forwards, through the water. The asymmetric tail compensates for the fact that sharks are heavier than water.

MOTHERLY COMFORTS

Most shark babies develop inside an egg, which is incubated inside a female shark. The mako shark, for example, uses this method. A few species of shark, including hammerheads, bull sharks and blue sharks grow inside the mother's womb, without the need of any kind of egg-sac, just like human babies.

Born in water
When sharks are born, they can swim and are ready to eat solid food.

Internal egg developers
Sand tiger sharks grow in an egg inside their mothers. Unlike blue sharks, which are fed through an umbilical cord, sand tiger sharks feed from a special yolk-sac in their egg.

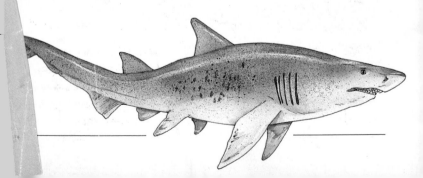

Skin

A shark's skin is rough because it is covered with tiny denticles. These small, hard scales have the same structure as a shark's teeth and are unique to sharks and rays. The shape of the denticles helps to identify some species of shark.

Second dorsal fin

Anal fin

Pelvic fin

Slimlined body

The body of many fast swimming sharks are flattened towards the back, which helps a shark to swim more speedily.

A SHARK'S MEAL

Meat-eating sharks are known to have huge and varied appetites. Although sharks prefer fish, shellfish and other marine life, sharks often swim behind boats and eat any rubbish that is thrown overboard. This complete menu was found inside a grey shark, nearly four metres in length, caught in Australian waters.

Menu

Starters

1 Piece of sacking

1 Ship's scraper

Main course

8 Legs of mutton

Half a ham

135 kilograms of horse flesh

Dessert

Head and forelegs of a bulldog

Hind quarters of a pig

TERROR OF THE DEEP?

You may believe that sharks are quick, silent and deadly hunters. This is often the image of sharks in films. But, although sharks live in all the world's oceans, not all of them are large, or indeed even dangerous. As we learn more about sharks, their fascinating lives and abilities, so we must also learn to respect and admire these graceful creatures.

A sailor's nightmare
Since the days of the earliest seafarers, sharks have been dreaded as evil and dangerous.

OLDER THAN DINOSAURS

The first sharks patrolled our seas about 400 million years ago, 100 million years before dinosaurs appeared. Some shark species eventually died out. Most of those that survived have changed very little in the last 200 million years. Sharks are such expert hunters, with so few enemies, that they simply have not needed to change.

The biggest shark

A shark called megalodon lived in the world's oceans until about 12,000 years ago. You can imagine how big megalodon was, by comparing the size of ourselves to just its jaw bones.

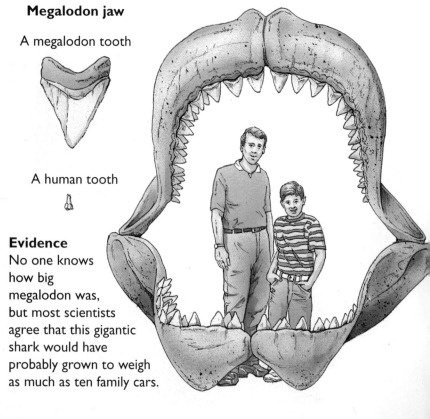

Megalodon jaw

A megalodon tooth

A human tooth

Evidence

No one knows how big megalodon was, but most scientists agree that this gigantic shark would have probably grown to weigh as much as ten family cars.

THE SHARK'S CLOSEST RELATIVES

Although they don't look like sharks, **rays** and **skates**, which swim with graceful, flapping 'wings', are closely related to sharks. So are the six species of sawfish and fifty species of guitarfish. Like all true sharks, the skeletons of all these fish are made not from bone, but **cartilage** – just like the bendy bits in your nose.

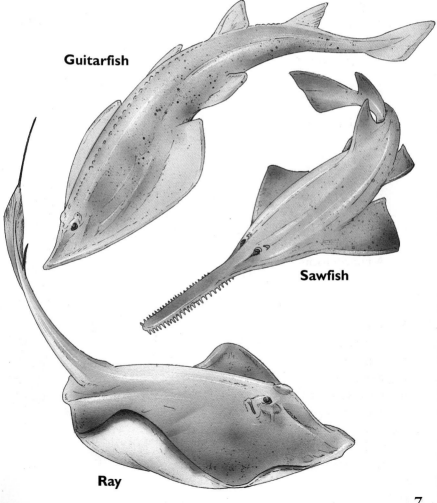

Guitarfish

Sawfish

Ray

STAYING AFLOAT

Sharks are heavier than seawater. This means that they could sink. But sharks' bodies have special adaptations. Sharks' livers contain oil, which is lighter than water, and so helps sharks to float. Also, some sharks gulp air into their stomachs, which provides extra buoyancy.

Shark skin
A shark's skin is covered in thousands of scales, called **denticles**, which point towards the tail. Rubbed from back to front, shark skin is very rough and so it was once used as **sandpaper**.

Caudal fin

Dorsal fin

Anal fin

Denticles
These are tiny tooth-like scales.

Pectoral fin

Gills

Teeth

A shark's body

A shark's skeleton

Most sharks are very **streamlined**. Their muscles are arranged in narrow zigzagging strips, which squeeze in and out as sharks swim. This gives sharks superb strength and speed in water and allows them to turn efficiently in tight circles.

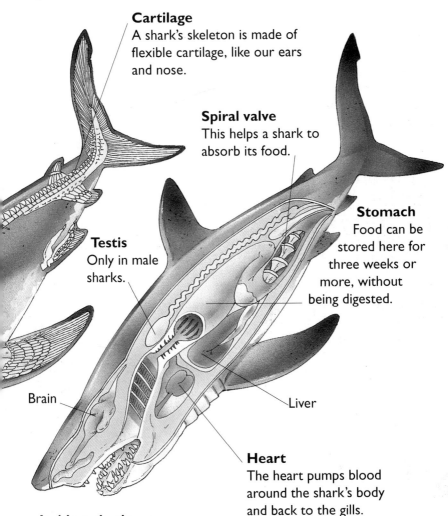

Cartilage
A shark's skeleton is made of flexible cartilage, like our ears and nose.

Spiral valve
This helps a shark to absorb its food.

Stomach
Food can be stored here for three weeks or more, without being digested.

Testis
Only in male sharks.

Brain

Liver

Heart
The heart pumps blood around the shark's body and back to the gills.

Inside a shark

WHAT FINE TEETH YOU HAVE!

Sharks' teeth come in different shapes and sizes, all designed for different jobs. What's more, there are several rows of teeth. When a tooth falls out, the tooth behind moves forward to take the previous tooth's place. On average sharks lose a tooth about once a week.

Slicing teeth
These are serrated to cut through flesh.

Spiked teeth
These are for gripping and tearing flesh.

Crushing teeth
These slab-shaped teeth are seen in sharks that feed on crustaceans on the sea floor.

Holding teeth
These long, sharp and pointed teeth help a shark to catch and hold on to slippery fish.

TAKING A BREATH

Like all fish, sharks have gills that draw **oxygen** from the water and pass it into the **bloodstream**. Shark gills are open slits – usually five of them – without the folding flap that other fish have. Most sharks need to keep swimming to ensure they receive a sufficient flow of water over their gills. Some, however, can breathe whilst remaining still.

Gill slits
As the shark swims, so water passes through the gill slits, which are like the arches in a bridge, through to the gills.

Slow sea floor swimmers
Not all sharks swim fast. Some, like the wobbegong, rest on the seabed. The spotted wobbegong moves from one rockpool to the next, searching for crabs and other crustaceans.

SHARK SENSES

A shark's senses are so acute that a shark can hear, smell and detect movements of **prey** from very far away. A shark's ears, for example, can pick up sounds more than one-and-a-half kilometres away. And if an injured fish starts to bleed, some sharks can smell the blood from 500 metres away – the length of five football pitches!

Shark eyes

A shark's eyes have a mirror-like layer that reflects the smallest amounts of light. This helps a shark to see, even in murky water. But, a shark cannot see as well as we can.

Shark ears

A shark's ears are inside its head, with tiny holes leading to the outside.

Sense of smell

A shark relies more on its sense of smell than its eyesight. A shark's nose and the front of its head are covered by tiny **pores** that can detect electrical impulses caused by the movements of other fish.

SENSES AT THE SIDES

A shark has a lateral line – tubes filled with a jelly-like substance – that runs down either side of a shark's body. These lateral lines sense vibrations caused by movement in water, within about 100 metres. The lines send nerve impulses to the brain and the shark reacts accordingly.

WHERE ARE THEY?

There are more than 370 species of shark in the world's seas. Sharks come in a wide variety of shapes, sizes and colours. Some sharks are wanderers, covering great distances, while others have their own small territories. Most sharks are found in warm seas – very few sharks live in cold water – although the blue shark has been found off the coast of Britain.

Tiger shark
This shark is ferocious by nature and prefers to swim in the top few hundred metres of the open sea. It occasionally moves inshore.

Goblin shark
This shark lives in the darkest and lowermost depths of the seas. Goblin sharks have been on the Earth for 70 million years. The long rod-like projection on its snout helps it to find food on the sea floor.

Blacktipped reef shark
This shark has a distinctive black **dorsal fin**. Like most shallow water sharks, it spends most of its life close to land, in water less than 200 metres deep.

Blue shark
This is a mid-water dweller – it rarely ventures near either the surface or the seabed.

WHITE DEATH

The great white shark, is the most dangerous of all sharks. In size, it is as long as a bus. Great white sharks are found in cool to warm waters. Their favourite meal is seal. Usually, they launch a surprise attack and take one huge bite of their victim then wait nearby for it to weaken before returning to finish the meal. These are the sharks that may attack people in shallow water, and drag them out to sea.

Great white shark
This shark will eat almost anything that comes along – smaller sharks, fish, penguins or even people.

HAMMERS AND BONNETS

No one knows why the hammerhead shark has such a strangely shaped head. Its widely-spaced eyes and nose, and its typically flat head may allow the hammerhead shark to sense and swim after prey more easily.

Hammerhead shark
This shark has hundreds of sensitive pores on the underside of its strangely shaped head. These pores may help the shark sweep the seabed more efficiently, to detect buried prey – like stingrays – one of its favourite meals.

Bonnet shark
Another member of the hammerhead group is the bonnet shark. From above, this shark's head resembles a car bonnet. Bonnet sharks hunt small fish and sea creatures such as crab and squid, often in shallow seas.

GENTLE GIANTS

The largest fish in the sea are the mighty whale shark and the basking shark. Yet neither of these giants are a threat to people. Instead of teeth, both have special filters in their gills that sieve tiny animals called **zooplankton** from the water.

The whale shark
This shark feeds during the day in the depths of warm tropical oceans. It grows to twelve metres and can weigh over twenty tonnes.

Surface skimmers

Some large sharks cruise slowly near the surface. Incredibly, they sometimes jump completely out of the water.

Basking shark

This shark can grow to be nearly fourteen metres long. About half a million litres of seawater flows through its gaping mouth every hour.

NEW SPECIES

In 1976 a rare, new shark was discovered – the megamouth. It was found tangled in the anchor of an American warship. Only a few megamouths have ever been caught. Very little is known about this shark, but it is thought to tempt prey into its huge, **luminous** mouth, which contains more than one hundred rows of teeth.
The megamouth lives in deep tropical waters.

MOVING RIGHT ALONG

Sharks are tailor-made for fast swimming. In fact, probably the only thing sharks cannot do, which most bony fish can, is swim backwards.

Streamlining

A shark's streamlined shape makes it very agile underwater and enables it to turn quickly. Also, its fins may curve slightly towards its tail, helping the animal to swim faster.

Fins for lifting

The **pectoral fins** act like an aeroplane's wings to help create 'lift' and move the shark up or down.

THE THRESHER SHARK

This shark's spine extends into the tail, giving it extra strength. The thresher shark's tail is actually longer than the whole of the rest of its body!

A rudder
A shark's tail sweeps from side-to-side like a **rudder**, pushing the shark through the sea.

Steering and turning
By moving its tail more to one side than the other, a shark can turn very sharply.

SHARK TAILS

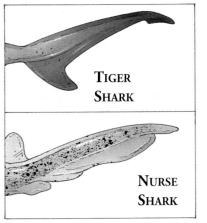

TIGER SHARK

NURSE SHARK

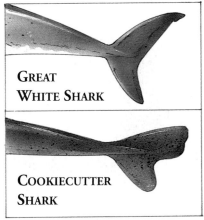

GREAT WHITE SHARK

COOKIECUTTER SHARK

SIX OF THE BEST KNOWN

Mako

This agile shark's high speed helps it to catch tuna and mackerel, its favourite foods. It swims near the surface and sometimes attacks boats, especially white boats.

Oceanic whitetip

A tuna may mistake the white tips of this shark's fins for small fish. When the tuna investigates, it finds itself lured into the shark's trap, and eaten.

Lemon shark

A young lemon shark can be aggressive towards divers, but the adult lemon shark is extremely shy. A lemon shark eats fish that live on the seabed.

Sand tiger shark

This shark's needle-sharp teeth make it look very fierce, but it is not a particularly dangerous one. In Australia it is called the grey nurse shark. It eats fish, smaller sharks, crabs and lobsters.

Leopard shark

This striking, black-spotted shark feeds mainly on clams. Common along the Pacific coast of North America, it is harmless to people.

Nurse shark

This large shark usually spends the day sitting on the seabed in shallow water. It sometimes attacks swimmers. At night it searches for crabs or small fish.

SIX WEIRD ONES

Frilled shark
This is a rare and primitive shark. Its gills create a frill that almost circles its head and looks like a collar. It lives in deep water and eats small fish, swallowing them whole.

Goblin shark
Until this shark was rediscovered near Japan, about a hundred years ago, the goblin shark was thought to be **extinct**. It lives near the bottom of the ocean.

Angel shark
This shark buries itself in sand or shingle, where it is well **camouflaged**. One kind of angel shark – the monkfish – is a popular food for us. It lives in the Mediterranean Sea and the Atlantic Ocean.

Cookiecutter shark

This is a small shark with strong jaws, that takes biscuit-shaped bites out of its prey – seals, whales and dolphins. The cookiecutter shark is sometimes called the cigar shark. It is very hard to catch, because it bites its way out of nets, using razor sharp teeth.

Spined pygmy shark

This is the smallest shark of all. It is also the only one with a spine on its dorsal fin.

Wobbegong

This shark has a ragged strip of skin that hangs over its mouth and looks like seaweed. When a creature investigates this fringe, the wobbegong strikes.

THE SHARK'S GREATEST ENEMY

Shark attacks on humans are nearly always caused by divers annoying the sharks, or by the sharks mistaking swimmers or surfers for their usual prey. Researchers have tried out many safeguards against attack, one being a tube-shaped inflatable container, called a shark screen.

Protection
Divers sometimes wear a **chain-mail diving suit** to keep themselves safe from sharks.

Shark cages
Divers use shark cages to protect themselves when studying sharks at close range. Films of sharks are also often photographed in this way.

Seal   Turtle   Surfer

Deciphering an outline
To a shark, the outline of a
person paddling on a surfboard
must be very similar to the
outline of a seal or turtle.

People kill a staggering
100 million sharks every year.
Sharks cannot survive such a high rate of slaughter,
especially as some of the larger species do not breed until
they are eighteen years old. Happily, some countries are
now actively trying to protect certain species.

**Killed for food
and sport**
Many sharks are killed
by the nets that protect
beaches. Sharks become
entangled in nets and drown.

AMAZING SHARK FACTS

● **River sharks**
Only two sharks may
sometimes leave the sea
and swim into freshwater
rivers. They are the bull
shark and the Ganges shark.

● **Light producing organ**
The lantern shark has small, special organs, set in its belly,
which produce light. The lantern shark lives deep in the Atlantic
Ocean, feeding on squid, crabs and similar creatures.

● **Cookiecutter sharks** These sharks swim about four
kilometres each day. They move up from the depths of the
ocean to feed near the surface.

● **White shark longevity** The great white shark may be the
most long-lived of all sharks. It is thought that individuals may
live for a hundred years.

● **The most common shark** The piked dogfish is thought to
be the most common shark in the world. Between 1904 and
1905, 27 million were caught off the American coast alone.
These sharks range widely through the world's oceans.

● **Having a ride** Remora fish stick very closely to sharks.
They use a special sucker pad to hitch a ride, anchoring
themselves to the shark's skin.

● **Horn shark eggs** Sharks' eggs come in
an assortment of shapes and sizes. One of the
strangest is the egg of the horn shark, which has
its own screwthread, enabling the mother
shark to fasten the egg securely in a
rocky crack.

● **Taking a look** Great whites lift
their heads out of the water to
look at objects on the surface.

GLOSSARY

Bloodstream The name for blood flowing round a body.

Camouflage The way in which a creature can conceal itself because of its appearance. It also usually lies still.

Cartilage The flexible substance of which sharks' skeletons are made.

Chain-mail diving suit Interlocking metal loops, like armour, which can save a diver from being badly attacked by a shark.

Denticles The tooth-like covering on a shark's skin, which gives it a rough feel.

Dorsal fin The fin on the shark's back. The dorsal fin becomes visible above the water when the shark is swimming close to the surface.

Extinct A creature which is thought to no longer exist on the planet.

Luminous An object which glows in the dark. Deep water sharks may have luminous areas on their bodies.

Oxygen A gas present in air and in water which is essential to life.

Pectoral fin The fin present just behind the head, on either side of a fish's body. These fins help the shark to change direction as it swims.

Pore A tiny opening in the skin, which allows liquid or air to pass through.

Prey Animals which are eaten by other animals.

Ray A wide-bodied fish, related to the shark.

Rudder The part of a boat, at the back, which is used for steering.

Sandpaper Paper, usually with grains of sand stuck to it, used to rub down wood and other surfaces to make them smooth.

Skate A group of fish related to sharks, which are often caught by people for food.

Streamlined Having a curved body which allows quick and easy movement through the water.

Zooplankton Tiny floating creatures which live in the oceans and are eaten by much larger animals, including some sharks.

INDEX *(Entries in **bold** refer to an illustration)*